THE SUN AND STARS

by Giles Sparrow

A⁺

Smart Apple Media

Published by Smart Apple Media
P.O. Box 3263, Mankato, Minnesota 56002

Printed in the United States of America at Corporate
Graphics, in North Mankato, Minnesota.

Published by arrangement with the
Watts Publishing Group Ltd., London.

Library of Congress Cataloging-in-Publication Data
Sparrow, Giles, 1970-
  The sun and stars / by Giles Sparrow.
    p. cm. -- (Space travel guides)
  Summary: "Describes the life story of a star,
introducing red giants, planetary nebulae,
supernovas, and black holes. Also discusses
different galaxies of the Universe, including the
Milky Way. Provides statistics and diagrams"--
Provided by publisher.
  Includes index.
  ISBN 978-1-59920-666-0 (lib. bdg.)
  1. Stars--Juvenile literature. 2. Sun--Juvenile
    literature. I. Title.
  QB801.7.S63 2012
  523.8--dc22

                                 2010039493

1021
3-2011

9 8 7 6 5 4 3 2 1

Conceived and produced by Tall Tree Ltd
Cartoons: Guy Harvey

Picture credits:
t-top, b-bottom, l-left, r-right, c-center
All images courtesy of NASA, except:
7tr Dreamstime.com/Girts Pavlins,
7br Dreamstime/Roman Krochuk

Disclaimer
The web site addresses (URLs) included in this book
were valid at the time of going to press. However,
because of the nature of the Internet, it is possible
that some addresses have changed, or sites may
have changed or closed down since publication.
While the author and publisher regret any
inconvenience this may cause to readers, no
responsibility for any such changes can be
accepted by either the author or the publisher.

This book describes a fictional journey into outer
space. It is not possible for humans to travel to
the inner planets with present-day technology.
Readers are invited to use their imaginations to
journey around our solar system.

Words in **bold** are in the glossary on page 30.

Contents

Twinkle, Twinkle

In this book, we're leaving Earth to travel past the Sun, across our **galaxy**, and finally out into the universe, looking at the countless different types of **stars** and other objects that fill the **cosmos**.

WHAT IS A STAR?

Stars are dense balls of gas that shine because of **nuclear reactions** in their central cores. While most objects in space (including planets such as Earth and **satellites** such as the Moon) shine only by reflecting light or sometimes by absorbing and re-emitting it, stars create their own energy and light. Stars come in a huge range of sizes. Some are barely the size of the **solar system's** largest **planet**, Jupiter, while others are so big they would engulf Jupiter's entire **orbit** around the Sun. Their brightness also varies greatly, from brilliant giants 100,000 times brighter than the Sun to weak dwarf stars (see page 19) 100,000 times fainter. A star's color is determined by its surface temperature, running through the whole rainbow from cool red and orange to scorching blue and violet.

BEYOND THE SUN

This book will take you on a journey around the cosmos, first to the Sun—our nearest star—and then through a whole range of objects that reveal the life story of a typical star. Finally, we'll take a look at our star-city, or galaxy, and venture many **light years** (1 light year is about 5.9 trillion miles, or 9.5 trillion kilometers) into the cosmos to look at the different types of galaxies that are out there.

Earth is one of eight planets in the solar system—a collection of astronomical bodies in orbit around our star, the Sun. Taking a look at the stars closest to the solar system reveals just some of the huge variety of stars in the universe.

THE SUN: *Our own star is yellow-white with a pretty average size and temperature.*
PROXIMA CENTAURI: *It might be the closest star to the Sun at just 4.2 light years, but Proxima Centauri is a feeble red dwarf star that is so faint you can only see its reddish light through a telescope!*
RIGEL: *With a mass some 17 times that of the Sun, this blue supergiant is the sixth brightest star in the sky. Located in the* **constellation** *of Orion, Rigel is also 40,000 times brighter than our star.*
ANTARES: *A massive red supergiant star, Antares is 800 times wider than the Sun.*
SIRIUS A: *The brightest star in the sky, it lies 8.6 light years from Earth. Sirius A is brilliant white with a surface almost twice as hot as the Sun, and it is twice the mass of the Sun.*
SIRIUS B: *This tiny white dwarf star orbits Sirius A every 50 years. It is hard to see its white light because of the brighter star's glare. It is all that is left of a star that was once much heavier, hotter, and brighter than even Sirius A.*

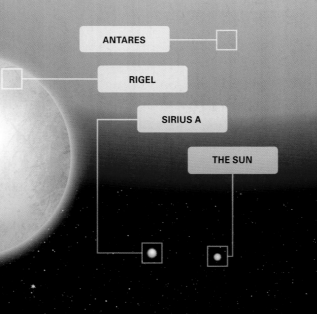

ANTARES

RIGEL

SIRIUS A

THE SUN

The Sun

1 The nearest star, the Sun, is 93 million miles (150 million km) from Earth. This huge ball of exploding gas, measuring 870,000 miles (1.4 million km) across, produces a blaze of heat and light that enables life to survive on our planet. But while it's essential to us, the Sun is really just an average star.

BLAZING FIREBALL

The Sun is too bright to look at directly, but special filters can help to show off some of its surface features. This reveals that the Sun has a surprisingly sharp edge—a layer called the photosphere where the burning gas suddenly becomes transparent. Light is created at the center of the Sun, but the interior is foggy and stops the light from getting out. The photosphere layer, with a temperature of around 9,930°F (5,500°C), is where the fog lifts and light escapes, allowing the Sun's surface features to become visible.

The Sun has a huge influence over the space around it. It pumps out more energy in a second than all of Earth's power plants would produce in 750,000 years. This energy spreads out as heat and light, keeping space within the inner solar system (out to around the orbit of Mars) fairly warm. The Sun's **gravity** trails off far more gradually than its energy. It traps planets and smaller objects in orbit out to about 1 light year away, a distance from which the Sun looks like just another star.

The Sun's rays warm Earth, sustaining life here. Plants convert the star's energy into food, and the Sun's heating effect on Earth's air and oceans drives our planet's climate and weather.

Huge jets of hydrogen gas shoot out at regular intervals from the Sun's surface.

THE SOLAR WIND

Light is not the only thing escaping from the solar surface. In addition, a blizzard of tiny electrically charged particles constantly blows away from the photosphere and out across the solar system. This solar wind is mostly invisible and can be harmful to space travelers. Some of its particles travel so fast that they will pass straight through an unshielded spaceship and through you! Planets with strong magnetic fields, such as Earth and Jupiter, trap solar wind particles. The fields funnel the particles toward the planet's north and south poles. Here, the particles collide with gases in the **atmosphere**, creating beautiful glowing patterns called aurorae, or the northern and southern lights. But watch out—there's a dangerous side to all this beauty in the form of deadly **radiation** belts that are also trapped by the magnetism!

Solar wind particles collide with Earth's magnetic field above the North Pole, creating swirling patterns of light.

Flares and Spots

From a distance, the Sun might look like a featureless disc, but up close, there's a lot going on. Look out for huge arcs of gas, or flares, looping out from the solar surface. You'll also see dark areas called sunspots, which can sometimes grow to the size of planets.

PROMINENCES AND SOLAR FLARES

Prominences are ever-changing loops of pinkish gas that hang near the Sun's surface. They are normally only visible through special filters or when the Sun's bright disc is blocked out—for example, when Earth's Moon passes in front of the Sun and eclipses it (see page 10). You can also see prominences silhouetted as dark lines against the bright photosphere. Solar flares are huge prominences that suddenly burst apart, flinging great clouds of gassy material out into the solar system at supersonic speeds.

Solar flares are massive explosions of gas in the atmosphere of the Sun, which release colossal amounts of energy into space. Most solar flares take place in regions around sunspots.

TRAVELER'S TIPS -
A SAFE WAY TO LOOK AT THE SUN

If you only take one piece of advice from this book, make sure it's this: NEVER try to look at the Sun directly. Even at the distance of Earth's orbit, it's brilliant enough to damage your eyesight permanently and is even more dangerous through binoculars or a telescope. In the early days of astronomy, many stargazers damaged their eyesight before learning the safe way to study the Sun. The only safe way to look at our star is by projecting its image onto a surface. To project the Sun's image, point a telescope at the Sun, but do not look through it. Instead, hold a piece of cardboard behind the eyepiece so that the Sun's disc appears on it.

SUNSPOTS

Sunspots are patches on the Sun's surface that look dark as they are much cooler (6,330°F or 3,500°C) than the surrounding area. Up close, they look like a pattern of iron filings disturbed by a magnet. This is because they are found at the end of huge loops of magnetism. Often a pair of sunspots is connected by such a loop with a prominence running along it. The number and size of sunspots, prominences, and flares change in an 11-year cycle as the Sun's magnetic field grows stronger and weaker.

Sunspots mark gaps in the photosphere as the loops of magnetism thin out the Sun's gas.

The Sun's Structure

The Sun's core is the key to its brilliance. The core is an enormous power plant that generates all the Sun's heat and light through nuclear reactions. It sends this energy on a 100,000-year journey to the Sun's surface.

NOT TO MISS

GRANULATION: *These cell-like patterns can be seen across the Sun's surface. They mark the tops of gas bubbles. The hot gas rises up in the bright center of each bubble, releases its energy, and then cools, sinking back down around the bubble's edges.*

SPICULES: *Towering pillars of flame the height of Earth (see below) carry energy from the photosphere into the upper reaches of the Sun's atmosphere.*

CHROMOSPHERE: *This cool region just above the visible photosphere forms a layer where pinkish loops of gas appear.*

TRANSITION REGION: *A mysterious layer above the chromosphere where the Sun's atmosphere is suddenly heated from about 5,000°F (3,000°C) to more than 1.8 million°F (1 million°C)*

CORONA: *The Sun's outer atmosphere; It extends for hundreds of thousands of miles (millions of kilometers) into space and blends into the solar wind.*

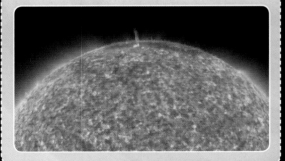

NUCLEAR FUSION

Deep inside the Sun, temperatures reach 27 million°F (15 million°C), and matter is compressed until it is 150 times denser than water. Most of the Sun's core is made from hydrogen gas, the lightest element. Pressure forces hydrogen atoms together to form the next lightest element, helium. This process is called nuclear fusion, and it creates enormous amounts of energy. Superheated gas, up to 3.6 million°F (2 million°C), streams into space to create the Sun's corona.

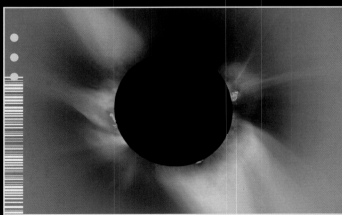

During a solar eclipse, the Moon passes between Earth and the Sun, blocking out the star's light. When this happens, the streams of hot gas that make up the Sun's corona, or outer atmosphere, can be seen with the naked eye.

JOURNEY TO THE TOP

Energy forces its way out of the Sun's core, but it has a long way to go to reach the surface. For tens of thousands of years, it bounces around in the dense solar interior, constantly colliding with particles of the Sun's gas and losing a little energy with each collision. Eventually, it reaches a point about 125,000 miles (200,000 km) below the surface where the energy is then carried upward over the course of a few days in huge bubbles. Near the Sun's surface, the energy is released from the top of the bubbles, escaping into space as heat and light.

The bubbles of hot gas escaping from the Sun give the star's surface layer, the photosphere, a grainy appearance. A typical bubble, or granule, measures 620 miles (1,000 km) in diameter.

The Birth of a Star

Stars are born in huge clouds of dust and gas, many light years across, called nebulae. Parts of these clouds are lit up by reflected starlight, but large, darker areas block out light beyond the nebulae. Once the process of star creation gets underway, however, a nebula can light up in a spectacular range of colors.

SLOW COLLAPSE

The process of star birth takes thousands of years. It starts when a small clump of gas and dust within a larger nebula gets compressed until it is dense enough to pull in material from all around it by gravity. More and more gas gets packed into a smaller space and grows hotter and hotter. Eventually, the heart of the collapsing cloud is so hot and dense that nuclear reactions begin, and a star is born. This is just how our Sun was born about five billion years ago.

The Orion Nebula is one of the brightest nebulae visible to the naked eye from Earth.

HELPING HANDS

Often, the process of star creation is triggered by other stars. The shockwaves from a massive exploding star called a supernova (see page 22) can push and pull gas within a nebula to form clumps of gas, which are the seeds of new stars. When these stars eventually ignite, strong stellar winds (just like our Sun's solar wind) can blow away material in the nebula around them. The new stars' fierce radiation can also cause the gas around them to glow in delicate colors.

NOT TO MISS

See if you can spot tiny, faint red dwarf stars that generate just enough power to shine. Also keep a look out for brown dwarfs—stars that never grew big enough to start proper nuclear reactions in the first place. Some of the best known are:

PROXIMA CENTAURI: *The closest star to the Sun and a faint red dwarf 600 times dimmer than the Sun*

BARNARD'S STAR: *Another nearby red dwarf that moves through space at 56 miles per second (90 km/sec) and is the fastest-moving star in Earth's skies*

GLIESE 229B: *The first brown dwarf to be discovered by astronomers, orbiting a faint red dwarf some 19 light years from Earth*

2M1207: *A brown dwarf that is orbited by its own planet, some 170 light years away from Earth*

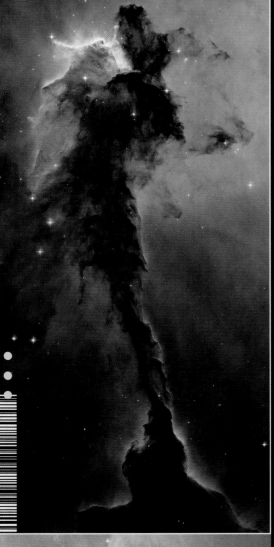

The Eagle Nebula contains huge columns of gas, which are separating to form ball-shaped clumps, or globules. In time, the cores of the globules will ignite to create new stars.

Proxima Centauri—a typical red dwarf—shines with a reddish light. The star is 4.2 light years from Earth.

Young Stars

Stars often take a long time to settle down after their birth. They emerge from their star birth nebulae surrounded by clouds of gas, which they need to get rid of in order to become stable. Stars form in **clusters** that slowly drift apart over millions of years.

OPEN CLUSTERS

Large groups of young stars are called "open clusters." They can contain dozens or even hundreds of individual stars, moving on more or less the same path through space but gradually separating. Open clusters are usually dominated by brilliant blue stars that far outshine average, Sun-like stars. However, these stellar heavyweights only live for a few million years before their fuel is exhausted. Only the more sedate, Sun-like stars make it out of the cluster and continue to shine for millions more years.

The Pleiades is one of the most well-known open clusters. It formed about 100 million years ago and is made up of about 1,000 young, blue-white stars.

GAS CLOUDS

A young star is still surrounded by a huge cloud of gas that is pulled inward by the star's gravity. Eventually, the star will not be able to absorb any more gas. As it grows heavier and heavier, it will spin faster and faster until finally any new gas falling onto the star will be flung off again instantly. This unwanted gas is usually funneled into jets, which shoot out from the star's poles. It can also billow out into beautiful glowing clouds as it gets farther away from the star.

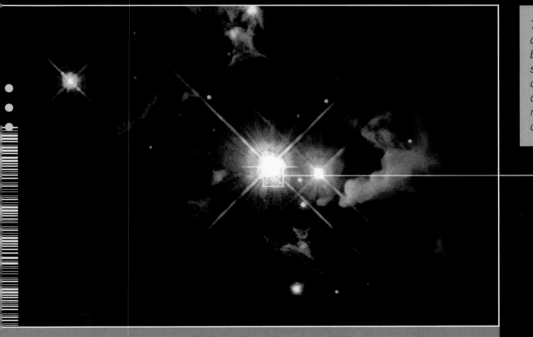

The young star at the center of this picture has blasted unwanted gas into space. The jets have collided with the remains of the original star-forming nebula, creating glowing clouds around the star.

Radiation from the star causes nearby gases to give off a pink glow. These gases, and the debris clouds above and below the star, are known as Herbig-Haro (HH) objects.

TRAVELER'S TIPS - BUILDING SIGHTS

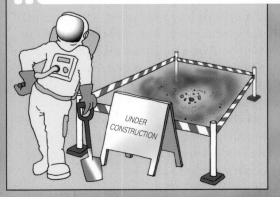

UNDER CONSTRUCTION

Watch out for solar systems under construction! As a young star finally settles down, it will be left with a disc of gas, frozen ice, and dust spinning around it. Close to the star, only dust can survive. These particles collide and stick together, forming clumps that may generate enough gravity to start pulling in more material, eventually growing into rocky planets like Earth. Farther out, there's much more gas and ice, and this tends to separate into huge orbiting fluffballs that slowly collapse to form giant gas planets like Jupiter and Saturn. There is always a lot of material left over, which tends to form rocky asteroids and icy comets.

Red Giants

After a stable middle age that can last for billions of years, a star will eventually run out of fuel for the nuclear reactions in its core. At this point, it will become unstable and change its size, brightness, and color, swelling into a brilliant star called a red giant.

KEEP ON BURNING

All stars spend their middle age burning the hydrogen gas in their cores to make helium (see page 10). When the hydrogen in the core is gone, however, the star begins to change. It now starts to burn hydrogen in a shell around the core. Eventually, the star begins to burn through the helium it has previously made, using a different nuclear reaction that makes other elements including carbon and oxygen. These changes make the star unstable.

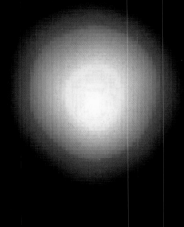

Between 300 and 400 times the diameter of our Sun, Betelgeuse is one of the brightest red giants that can be seen from Earth. The giant star has a visible, central hot spot and a thin outer shell of hydrogen gas.

TRAVELER'S TIPS - DON'T GET FRIED!

SUNSCREEN

How long do we have before the Sun turns into a red giant? The lifespan of any star depends on how heavy it is, and in this case, we're lucky that our local star is a comparative lightweight. Blue-white stars much heavier than the Sun have much more fuel to burn in the first place, but they shine so much more brightly that they get through it all in just a few million years. In contrast, our steady-burning yellow star has enough hydrogen to keep shining steadily for another five billion years. Eventually, though, it too will turn into a red giant, probably engulfing the planets Mercury and Venus and burning Earth to a crisp. If we're still around at the time, we'll have to move farther out in the solar system in order to survive.

Even though its main fuel supply is gone, the new nuclear reactions in an elderly star actually mean it gets much brighter than it was before. With more radiation pushing out, the star's upper layers billow outward. Eventually, a red giant can grow to millions of miles (hundreds of millions of kilometers) across. As the star's surface gets ever more thinly spread, it cools down and its color changes from yellow, blue, or white to cooler orange or red.

The massive star Eta Carinae is hidden from view by the Homunculus Nebula, a debris cloud made up of two lobes produced in a violent eruption by the unstable star in the 1840s.

Planetary Nebulae

 Most red giants end their lives by puffing off their outer layers into space, creating a glowing cloud of expanding gas called a planetary nebula. These nebulae have nothing to do with planets, but their cosmic smoke rings look spherical and planet-like.

THE END OF A RED GIANT

As a red giant nears the end of its life, it reaches a point where it has no more fuel to burn. It starts to pulsate, expanding and contracting until it expands so much that its outer layers fly off into space. Energy from the star itself keeps these ring-like clouds shining for thousands of years. They eventually fade, and the cast-off elements in the nebula form raw material for new stars. At 700 light years away, the Helix Nebula (right) is one of the closest planetary nebulae to Earth.

COMPLEX PLANETARIES

Not all planetary nebulae form a neat spherical shell around their star. Many, such as the Cat's Eye Nebula, get twisted into amazing shapes by powerful forces such as the star's rotation or its magnetic field. One of the most familiar types of complex planetary nebula has an hourglass shape with a pinch in the middle and bulges in two directions. The pinch may be caused by the presence of a smaller star, a large planet, or a ring of dust orbiting close to the main star.

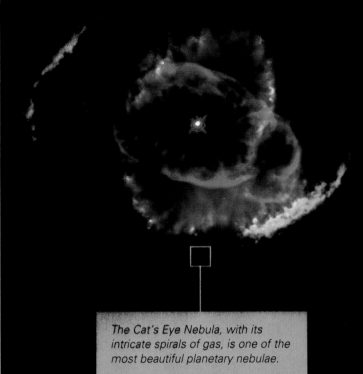

The Cat's Eye Nebula, with its intricate spirals of gas, is one of the most beautiful planetary nebulae.

LITTLE HEAVYWEIGHTS

As a red giant throws off its outer layers and stops producing new energy through nuclear reactions, its core—heated to millions of degrees—continues to shine. The white-hot remains of an old star may still weigh as much as the entire Sun. With no energy source to support them against their own weight, they slowly collapse inward, until eventually the atoms are jammed tightly against each other. These white dwarf stars may contain the mass of the Sun in a sphere the size of the Earth. Or, to put it another way, a matchbox-full of white dwarf matter could weigh as much as a fully-grown elephant. Billions of years from now, the Sun itself will also end its life as a slowly cooling white dwarf.

The brightest star in our sky is the white star Sirius A. Its tiny companion star, Sirius B, is a roughly Earth-sized white dwarf with a mass similar to that of the Sun.

Strange Stars

Stars vary a lot from one another in size, weight, brightness, and color. Many stars spend their lives orbiting one another in pairs or bigger groups. Most stars pass through phases where they fluctuate, changing their size and brightness in regular cycles.

DOUBLES AND MULTIPLES

Stars in pairs and groups may seem strange to us. In fact, most stars in the galaxy are binary pairs or multiples, and it is single stars like the Sun that are the minority. Stars within a group usually form at the same time and from the same chunk of nebula. The differences we often see between stars in a system are a big clue to how a star's size affects its lifespan. The more massive a star is, the faster it ages.

The Trapezium is a small star cluster in the Orion Nebula. Each of the five huge, bright young stars at the heart of the Trapezium shines brighter than 10 million Suns.

VARIABLE STARS

Most stars that vary their brightness do so because they are in unstable phases of their lives. These variable stars are often very young or very old, and they fluctuate in size as well as brightness. Sometimes, two stars in orbit around each other might be so close together that they look like a single star from Earth. The truth may only be revealed when one star blocks out or eclipses the other and the amount of light reaching Earth drops.

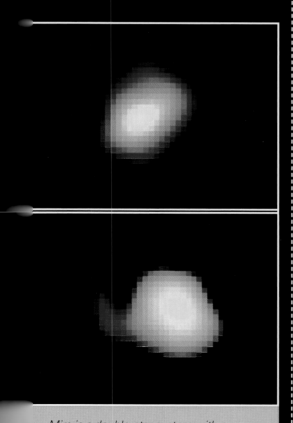

Mira is a double-star system with a massive, fluctuating red giant, called Mira A (above top). Material is pulled away from Mira A by tiny Mira B, forming a disc around the smaller star (above bottom).

NOT TO MISS

Astronomers have detected planets orbiting around distant stars. The existence of each alien world was revealed when the planet passed in front of its star, eclipsing, or blocking out, some of the star's light. The best known of these alien solar systems are:

PSR 1257+12: *This unusual planetary system contains at least three planets of different sizes orbiting a fast-spinning pulsar (see page 24), the burnt-out remains of a star that went supernova.*

51 PEGASI: *Just one planet is known to orbit this Sun-like star 50 light years from Earth. It was the first planet to be discovered around a normal star beyond our solar system.*

TAU BOOTIS: *A scorching planet, far more massive than Jupiter, orbits this star every 3.3 days while a red dwarf companion star orbits much farther out.*

FOMALHAUT: *This brilliant star is one of the brightest in the sky. It lies 25 light years from Earth and is surrounded by a ring of warm dust (see below) with a planet orbiting on its inside edge.*

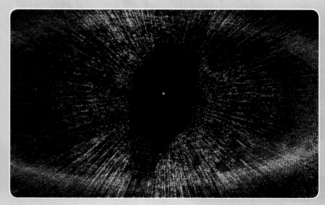

Supernovae

Not all stars end their lives as planetary nebulae and white dwarfs. Rare giant stars with more than eight times the mass of our Sun have a much more spectacular ending. They die in an explosion called a supernova, which can be bright enough to outshine an entire galaxy!

SUPERGIANT TO SUPERNOVA

Heavyweight stars that are close to the end of their lives swell into enormous supergiants that are about ten times bigger than a normal red giant. When the last of the fuel runs out and the reactions stop, the star's core weighs so much that it collapses inward in a fraction of a second. This creates a shockwave that rebounds and rips through the star's outer layers. The shockwave compresses and heats the star's outer layers so that they ignite, creating the blazing light of a supernova.

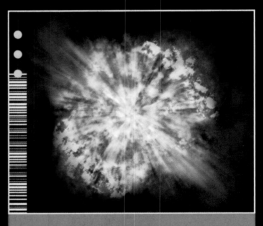

As a supergiant's core collapses, the huge release of energy blasts through the star, igniting the outer layers of gas.

TRAVELER'S TIPS - SOWING THE SEEDS

Supernovae play a unique role in sowing the seeds of life across the cosmos. The matter blasted across space in supernova explosions is believed to be the source of all heavy elements: the rocks and metals that form a small but important part of every solid planet, including Earth. They are also a part of every living creature, including ourselves. We're all made up of stardust! Matter from supernova explosions gets caught up in interstellar nebulae, where it lies waiting—often for millions of years—for the next round of star formation. The eventual star birth may itself be triggered by the shockwave ripples from another supernova.

SHREDDED REMAINS

On average, one star in our galaxy goes supernova every century or so. These brilliant beacons only shine for a few weeks before fading away. However, the star's outer layers, heated to enormous temperatures, continue to expand for thousands of years as a glowing cloud called a supernova remnant. The brightest remnant in Earth's skies is the Crab Nebula, the remains of a star that went supernova in the year 1054. Today, these glowing shreds of gas have expanded across 10 light years of space and are still heated to 32,400°F (18,000°C).

At 6,300 light years away, the sprawling Crab Nebula supernova remnant has expanded over a vast distance. The energy it gives out is equivalent to about 750,000 Suns.

Neutron Stars and Black Holes

The cores of heavyweight stars are compressed by enormous forces at the moment of a supernova explosion, producing some of the oddest objects in the universe. Super-dense neutron stars form pulsating cosmic lighthouses, and awe-inspiring black holes gobble up anything that comes near them—even light!

NEUTRON STARS

In some massive stars, the collapse of the core is so sudden and powerful that the tiny particles that make up its atoms get jammed together to form neutrons, which can be packed together very tightly. A neutron star may have the mass of many Suns in a city-sized space. It is so dense that a pinhead of matter would weigh as much as a fully laden oil supertanker.

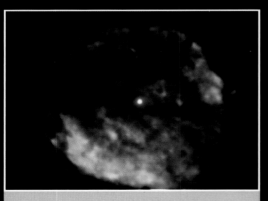

This superdense neutron star is known as G11.2-0.3. It is located some 16,000 light years from Earth.

NOT TO MISS

Collapsed neutron stars often form rapidly spinning pulsars. These stars emit nearly all their energy in a tightly focused beam that sweeps across the sky as the pulsar itself rotates at very high speeds. Some of the best-known pulsars include:

PSR 1919+21: The first pulsar to be discovered, in 1967; At first astronomers thought its regular radio pulses might be a signal from aliens, so they nicknamed it LGM-1 (short for "Little Green Man").

THE CRAB PULSAR: The pulsar at the heart of the Crab Nebula (see below); It was left behind by a supernova that exploded 1,000 years ago (see page 23).

PSR J1748-2446AD: This is the fastest-spinning pulsar on record, spinning 716 times every second.

BLACK HOLES

If a star's collapsing core weighs more than five Suns, its collapse will not stop at the neutron star stage. Instead, the neutrons are smashed together into even smaller particles and the core collapses to a single point in space. Gravity around the core gets so strong that beyond a frontier called the event horizon, nothing can escape it—not even light, the fastest-moving thing in the universe. The star has become a black hole and will pull in anything that gets too close, so keep your distance!

A black hole has a dark appearance because it absorbs all the light that hits it, reflecting nothing. The collapsed star is surrounded by swirling gas and dust drawn in by its gravity.

Our Galaxy

Our galaxy, the Milky Way, is a huge cloud of gas, dust, and about 200 billion stars, spinning in a spiral with a bright bulge at its center. The solar system lies roughly two-thirds of the way from the center to the outer edge in the space between two of the major spiral arms.

BAND OF STARS

When we look into space from inside the Milky Way, we can see dense star clouds lying in front of each other, forming a band across the sky. This is the galactic plane—a side-on view of the galaxy. To the naked eye, stars in this band blend together to create the pale, milky light that gives our galaxy its name. The clouds are brightest near the constellation of Sagittarius, toward the galaxy's densely packed center. Dark patches in the Milky Way are caused by dust clouds blocking out light.

The thin red band in the center of the star field shows the galactic plane as it appears in the constellation of Sagittarius.

TRAVELER'S TIPS - THE SIZE OF THE MILKY WAY

The Milky Way is so huge that it is almost impossible to grasp its size. In fact, astronomers used to think that it made up the whole universe! From edge to edge, the Milky Way is 100,000 light years across, which is so huge that a spacecraft traveling at the fastest speed reached by the Apollo Moon missions (about 25,000 mph or 39,500 km/h) would take 2.7 billon years to cross it. In fact, the galaxy is so big that even with 200 billion stars, most are spread out so widely that they are an average of 5 light years apart. That's still more than 100,000 years of travel for an Apollo-speed spaceship!

Seen from outside, this overhead view of the galaxy shows its multi-armed spiral shape with the arms linked to the central bulge by a short bar of stars. Astronomers believe that an enormous black hole, with the mass of millions of Suns, lies at the heart of the galaxy. The spiral arms are marked out by bright star-forming nebulae and short-lived clusters of brilliant stars that are constantly being replaced.

Stars circle around the galactic center in slow orbits. Our solar system (indicated by the pointer) is near the galaxy's outer edge. The Sun takes 230 million years to complete one orbit.

Other Galaxies

The Milky Way is just one galaxy among many in the Universe. Astronomers think there may be 200 billion galaxies. Most are separated by millions of light years, but large galaxies, such as ours, often have small satellite galaxies orbiting like moons around a planet.

GALAXY TYPES

Galaxies come in a range of shapes and sizes. About a quarter are spirals, and some of these have a bar of stars across the middle like our Milky Way. The shape, brightness, and number of spiral arms change from galaxy to galaxy. About two-thirds of the galaxies in the universe are ellipticals. These balls of stars can be much bigger or smaller than spirals and are packed with old yellow and red stars. The rest are irregular galaxies—shapeless clouds of gas and dust rich in star birth nebulae and young blue stars.

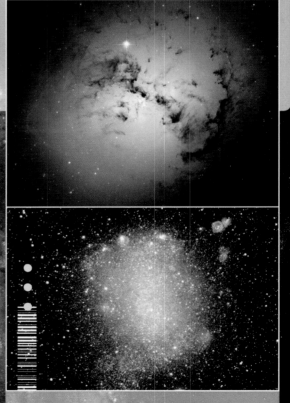

The Pinwheel (shown left) is a swirling spiral galaxy; Fornax A (above top) has a hub but no spiral arms; Barnard's Galaxy (above bottom) is a shapeless irregular galaxy.

VIOLENT GALAXIES

Some galaxies have cores that blaze with far more light than their surrounding stars and produce huge jets blasting out into intergalactic space. These active galaxies come in various types, but all have the same objects at their cores—gigantic black holes weighing more than a million Suns each and gobbling up everything around them. These belch out huge amounts of energy and excess matter, heating the surrounding region.

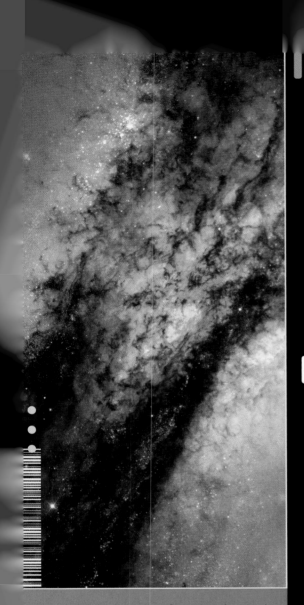

The elliptical active galaxy Centaurus A recently collided with a smaller spiral galaxy. The dark dust lane across the middle of the picture shows where the spiral galaxy was absorbed.

The unwound spiral arms of the Antennae galaxies resemble long, antenna-like streams.

NOT TO MISS

LARGE MAGELLANIC CLOUD: *The brightest of the Milky Way's satellite galaxies, the "LMC" is home to a vast star birth region called the Tarantula Nebula.*

ANDROMEDA GALAXY: *The nearest major galaxy to our own, Andromeda is a huge spiral 2.5 million light years away, just visible with the naked eye from Earth.*

CIGAR GALAXY: *This irregular galaxy, roughly 15 million light years away, is going through a huge "starburst"—a spasm of star formations that makes it look as though the entire galaxy is exploding.*

STEPHAN'S QUINTET: *This is an elegant group of five large galaxies, including four that are trapped in orbit around one another. The fifth just happens to lie in the same direction when seen from Earth.*

ANTENNAE GALAXIES: *The spiral arms of these two galaxies have unwound as a result of a cosmic collision, while the head-on impact between their cores has triggered a huge wave of star formation.*

Glossary

Atmosphere
The thin band of gases around a planet or a moon

Clusters
Collections of stars or galaxies moving together through space

Constellation
An area of the sky containing stars and other astronomical objects; Some groups of stars within a constellation may appear to form a pattern in the sky.

Cosmos
The universe and all it contains, from planets and stars to galaxies, black holes, neutron stars, and nebulae

Galaxy
A vast number of star systems held together by gravitational attraction; Our galaxy is called the Milky Way.

Gravity
The force of attraction that astronomical bodies exert on each other as a result of their masses; The more massive they are, the stronger the gravitational force.

Light year
A unit used to measure the vast distances of space; The distance traveled by light in one year is roughly 5.9 trillion miles (9.5 trillion kilometers).

Nuclear reaction
The process in which the nucleus (core) of an atom is changed by interacting with the nucleus of another atom

Orbit
The curved path of one astronomical object around another as a result of gravitational attraction

Planet
An object that follows its own orbit around a star and is massive enough to be rounded into a spherical shape by its own gravity

Radiation
Energy given off by a body such as a star; A star's light is a form of radiation.

Satellites
Objects that orbit, or travel around, another larger body; Natural satellites include the moons orbiting the planets.

Solar system
The family of objects in orbit around the Sun, including eight major planets and small bodies such as comets

Star
A massive ball of gas held together by gravity; Its core is hot and dense enough to trigger nuclear reactions that release energy, causing the star to shine.

Resources

BOOKS

Beyond the Solar System : from Red Giants to Black Holes
by Steve Parker
Earth and Space
(Rosen Central, 2008)

Stars—Birth and Death
Explore the Universe
(World Book, Inc., 2010)

The Sun
by George Capaccio
Space!
(Marshall Cavendish Benchmark, 2010)

The Universe
Space Frontiers
by Helen Whittaker
(Smart Apple Media, 2011)

QUICK QUIZ

Here are three quick-fire questions to test your knowledge on the Sun and the stars. (Answers at the bottom) Good luck!

1. How big is the Sun's diameter? Is it:
 a) 870,000 miles (1.4 million km)
 b) 6.2 million miles (10 million km)
 c) 12.7 million miles (20.5 million km)

2. What is a nebula made up of? Is it:
 a) planets
 b) galaxies
 c) dust and gas

3. What type of star is known as a cosmic lighthouse? Is it:
 a) a red giant
 b) a pulsar
 c) a white dwarf

WEB SITES

www.universetoday.com
Space exploration and astronomy news brought to you from around the Internet

www.nasa.gov/audience/forstudents
Scientists from NASA (National Aeronautics and Space Administration) answer your questions on the solar system and the universe.

www.spaceplace.nasa.gov/en/kids
Out-of-this-world space puzzles, quizzes, and activities to test your knowledge

http://starchild.gsfc.nasa.gov/docs/StarChild/
This learning center for young astronomers offers two levels of information, videos, and activities for students to enjoy.

www.sciencewithme.com
A variety of resources about space exploration and spaceflight; Includes many interactive and 3D animated views

www.kidsastronomy.com
A comprehensive guide to the universe with interactive features and games

Quiz Answers: 1. a 2. c 3. b

Index